Workbook

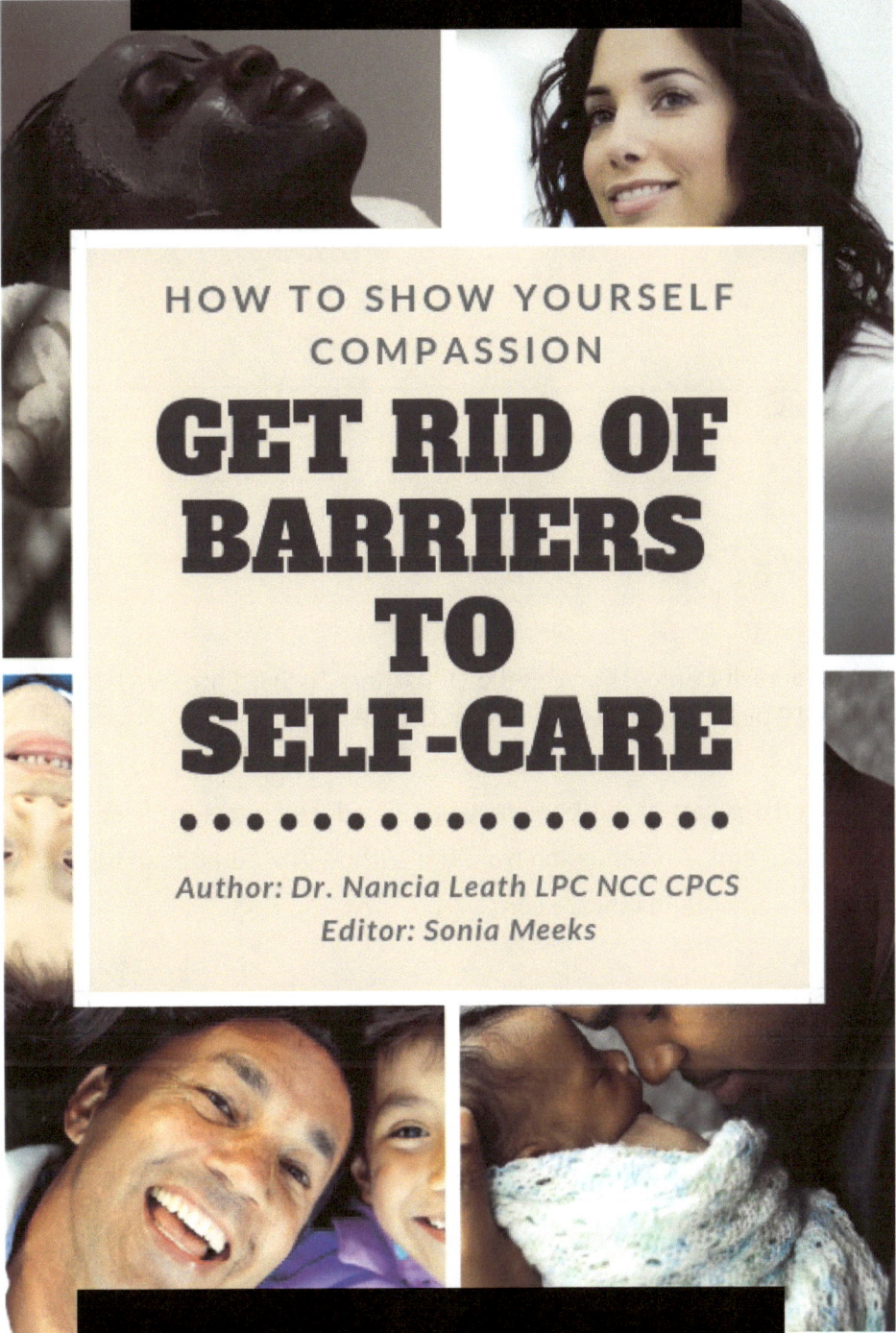

HOW TO SHOW YOURSELF COMPASSION

GET RID OF BARRIERS TO SELF-CARE

· · · · · · · · · · · · · · · · · ·

Author: Dr. Nancia Leath LPC NCC CPCS

Editor: Sonia Meeks

7 WEEKS

TABLE OF **CONTENTS**

 TAKE TIME TO PRAY

 WORKOUT

 SPEND TIME WITH FRIENDS

 SING IN THE SHOWER

 JOIN SUPPORT GROUPS

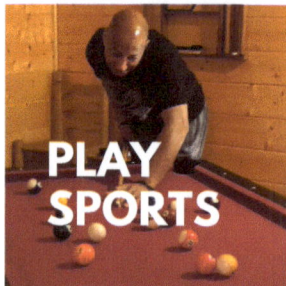 PLAY SPORTS

 ATTEND THERAPY SESSION

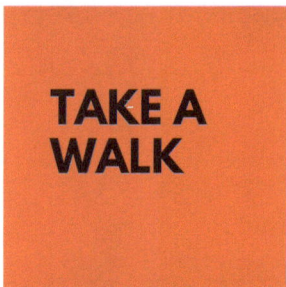 TAKE A WALK

 ATTEND A GAME

 EATING OUT

 ENJOY OUTDOORS

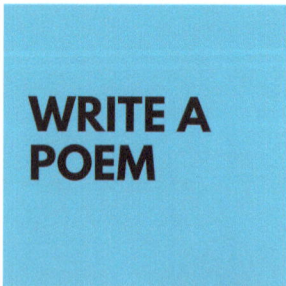 WRITE A POEM

 GO SHOPPING

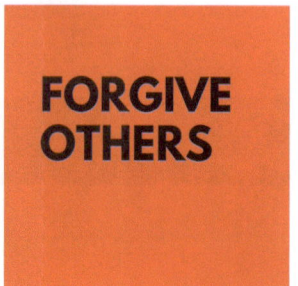 FORGIVE OTHERS

INTRODUCTION

Self-care is becoming very popular concept on social media. Many people are beginning to realize that it's time to take better care of themselves. They are no longer cutting back on socializing, exercising, traveling, or skipping meals. Why? Because people understand that self-care is crucial for their spiritual, physical, emotional and mental well-being. Lack of self-care can be the cause of people maintaining dangerous levels of stress, burnout, and even sickness. Although there are some who have already jumped on the self-care bandwagon, there are many who feel guilty, don't believe they have the time, just don't know how, or are expecting or waiting for others to do it for them.

Many books and internet blogs offer ways to exercise self-care. This workbook is going to allow you to work on removing obstacles that are preventing you from practicing self-care.

You will learn why you are still experiencing stress even after going on that great vacation, getting eight hours of sleep, practicing gratitude, working out, coloring, spending time with friends, or going to the spa. You may do things to show you are caring for yourself, but it's not impacting you in ways you need to recover. This book will show you how to prepare your mindset for self-care. So let's enjoy the process.

Self Care

SPEND TIME WITH THOSE YOU LOVE AND LOVE YOU

SELF-CARE

Self-care is purposely taking time to pay attention to your emotional, spiritual, physical, and mental needs to be healthy and enjoy life. Simply put, self-care is making sure you are being cared for by you.

SELF CARE – Day 1

On the seventh day, God rests according to the Bible in Genesis 2:1-3. It wasn't because he was tired according to Psalm 147:5. God was never tired, and He never needed to rest. The meaning of rest in this verse means to stop. God decided to stop creating on the seventh day. Today many religions encourage people not to work, but to rest at least one day within the week. Some people consider Sunday as the first day to rest. Others rest on the seventh day, which they consider Saturday and some don't rest at all. When you participate in self-care, it is essential that you stop or rest. Take time to rest and take care of yourself.

What can you do for yourself to stop or rest, to show yourself self-care?

Spiritually?

_____
_____
_____
_____
_____
_____

Mentally?

_____
_____
_____
_____
_____
_____

Physically?

_____
_____
_____
_____
_____
_____

Emotionally?

_____
_____
_____
_____
_____
_____

Now that you have identified what needs to be done to care for yourself in these areas, it's time to remove the barriers that are stopping you. Before we physically take action steps, close your eyes and ask God to help, to guide and forgive you for not showing yourself compassion in all areas of your life.

_____

_____

SELF CARE – Day 2

Take time to forgive yourself. To begin self-care, we must remove barriers by forgiving ourselves from things, experiences or situations. For example, forgive yourself for not showing yourself compassion, for procrastination, for living off excuses, or loving others or things more than yourself, etc. Nothing is too small or big to forgive yourself on today.

Today I forgive myself for

_____
_____
_____
_____

Today I forgive myself for

_____
_____
_____
_____

Today I forgive myself for

_____
_____
_____
_____

Today I forgive myself for

_____
_____
_____
_____

Today I forgive myself for

_____
_____
_____
_____

Today I forgive myself for

_____
_____
_____
_____

SELF CARE – Day 3

Pain from your past will prevent you from expressing, enjoying, or gaining relief in showing yourself self-care. You are carrying over negative experiences and people from your past. Today it is time to let yesterday go. You will only need the days of old to help you learn from, but not maintain offenses or grudges. Today it is time to have a death ceremony for all your bad and sad experiences. Write down below everything you dislike that happened in your life. It doesn't matter if you were the cause for the outcome, today you chose to move forward in your life.

Today I_____ let go of _____
_____
_____
_____
_____
_____
_____
_____
_____
_____
_____

Write down what you learned and what you are thankful for from those experiences
_____
_____
_____
_____
_____
_____
_____
_____

Say aloud

 "I let go of the pain of my past that caused me to live in unforgiveness, bitterness, jealousy, nightmares or any negative feelings. I've decided to no longer allow those emotions to lead me or influence my actions towards myself or others. Today I see myself taking off the chains and see myself free. My story has changed on today. I forgive myself, I release all my pain, and if thoughts from my past come to remind me of those bad feelings, I will also remind myself of how I let those things go and those situations, nightmares are no longer mine. I am FREE! Today I chose to smile, dance, sing, love, care for myself and those who will allow me to."

Now tell someone whom you respect or post on your social media of how you decided to become free to help seal your deal to yourself and maintain accountability.

Take time to read your Bible and books to help feed and grow this decision. Please stay away from movies, books, conversations, or anything that will try to motivate you to override your decision.

SELF CARE – Day 4

Close your ears and emotions to people who say things that cause you to feel down emotionally. Doing this is how you breakthrough your walls of discouragement. Most people encourage you to remove those people out of your life. However, there are some people you don't want to let go of because you love or need them. Such as your mom, father, or supervision. The great thing is you have the power to stop them and keep them in your life. Write down a list of people who make you feel bad about yourself because of how they may speak to you or view you.

_____

_____

_____

_____

_____

_____

Now that you have identified people you will no longer listen to their words of discouragement and stop them let's start by forgiving and then pray a blessing towards them. When you pray for them, it will help get rid of any forms of offenses.

Take time to learn their story to understand why before being negative towards you, so you make them human, because we realize that humans usually reciprocate feelings. Plus we all know the famous saying "people who are hurt tend to hurt people," even if they love or care for them. This will allow you not to maintain offense, help you ignore their words, and also take active steps to stop them. The key is making sure you prevent them from a place of protecting yourself, without causing the same type of harm.

How to stop them.
1. Let them know the words they use to cause you harm. Make sure you say the words in the format in how they may use the words. Explain how powerful their words are and how you will never want anyone to speak to them that way.
2. Tell them they will need to stop and you will no longer accept it because you respect yourself.
3. Thank them for no longer talking down to you.

If the person ignores your request or tries to judge you for speaking up for yourself, please know that's normal. Please do what's needed to make sure you don't become offended by their responses. The next time you see him/her act as though nothing happened with confidence. Please know your words are going to be with him/her when you two depart. How you responded is going to cause him/her to examine themselves. If he/she does it again, you repeat steps 1-3. Please-know it takes some people longer to break bad habits. It's not your fault, but stand your ground with kindness and respect for yourself and the person you are addressing. You are no longer allowing yourself to be their victim. You are also making sure their behaviors do not emotionally trigger you. Nor mirroring their behaviors to cope.

SELF CARE – Day 5 -7

Read over day 1 – 4 from this week and think about what you can do this weekend for yourself to help you celebrate strengthening your inner core. You did a lot of work this week to better yourself by completing SELF CARE days 1-4. Don't get too excited because you're just getting started and there is more work for you to do. Still, take time to celebrate yourself. If you like, consider selecting an activity from the Self-Care Action Steps section on pages 27 -30 out of the book "How To Show Yourself Compassion - Get Rid Of Barriers To Self-Care." Please answer the questions below.

What did you decide to do? _____

Which day(s) are you going to do it? _____

How do you think taking care of yourself this way will benefit you?
_____
_____
_____
_____
_____
_____
_____
_____
_____
_____

What do you believe about yourself on today (state a short affirmation)?
_____
_____
_____
_____
_____

Please repeat this affirmation all weekend and the following week to help you believe it from your heart and not just in your mind.

Remember to open this workbook on Monday to start the next lesson, enjoy your weekend!!

Know
Your
Value!

KNOW YOUR VALUE – Day 1

What are you doing as evidence that you value yourself?

Spiritually?

_____
_____
_____
_____
_____
_____

Mentally?

_____
_____
_____
_____
_____
_____

Physically?

_____
_____
_____
_____
_____
_____

Emotionally?

_____
_____
_____
_____
_____
_____

State how you will value yourself more in these areas and why below.

_____
_____
_____

KNOW YOUR VALUE – Day 2

Take time to write about why you are valuable.

I'm valuable because

_____
_____
_____
_____

After reading Know Your Value on page 13-14 out of the book, why is it important that you understand your motivation for self-care?

_____
_____
_____
_____

When can putting yourself first become selfish?

_____
_____
_____
_____

When can putting yourself last become wrong?

_____
_____
_____
_____

Why is it important to have balance when showing yourself self-care?

_____
_____
_____
_____

Say aloud
"I _____ am valuable because I've been made in God's image. I am not a god in any way, but my creator has given me value. It is recorded in the Bible he has prepared a table for me in the presence of my enemies, which shows he values me even when others around me may not. I am valuable because GOD said so and not what I or others believe about me. Today, tomorrow, and forever I will be valuable regardless of what I do or say. I chose to believe this is true."

WORKBOOK for How To Show Yourself Compassion - Get Rid Of Barriers To Self-Care. (KNOW YOUR VALUE)

KNOW YOUR VALUE – Day 3

Now that you understand that you will always be valuable, it is time for you to identify the things you lack. Before you do, please understand because you are to God, he will never withhold good things from you. Did you know that being created by God you are worthy of companionship, affection, attention, kindness, freedom, respect, peace, health, abundance, joy, and most of all, love? YES!!! However, he gives us free will and your choices, plus outside sources you may not be able to control may cause a lack in your life. Today you can take steps to changing that in your life, by changing your beliefs, creating goals, taking healthy actions steps, and believing God ~~is~~ are with you. You are worthy of having what you need in your life because you were created by God. It has nothing to do with who you are, your parents, skin color, or gender. Let's start-by changing your belief system.

Today I_____ believe I can have _____
_____
_____
_____
_____

I will not take it from anyone, but do what's needed to earn all these things by trusting God to lead and direct me. I believe God will put people in my life and setup situations for me to thrive in all areas of my life. I give up the feelings of _____
_____
_____
_____

These feelings are causing me not to take steps to accomplish my goals, but today I let them go, because I'm worthy to have what God has created for me. I will not put any of these things before him, but thank him for giving me value and making me worthy, In Christ Jesus name, I seal this prayer.

Now it's time for you to create your goals and take action steps. If you need assistance, motivation, and will like to be a part of a closed private Life Coaching Group, send an email to info@inwardcorehealthcare.com.

KNOW YOUR VALUE – Day 4

Now that you understand your value, it is also important to value others in the world. Some of us have been encouraged or trained not to appreciate others existence because of their skin color, gender, money status, sexuality, stereotypes, criminal record, or how they may live. We justify devaluing others when they don't meet our expectations or think as we do. In order to prevent selfishness when showing self-care and benefit from it emotionally, it is imperative that we view all people equally no matter our differences. Name different people you don't value and why. It could be your father who abandoned you or that person who works with you, but you consider her to be a slacker. State that person name below and your why below

_____

_____

_____

_____

_____

Now that you have identified people and your reason why devalue them think about how people decided to devalue you. If you are honest you know that doesn't feel good and it's not the right way to think concerning anyone that's different. Especially when God created all people in his image and made us all valuable and worthy. Today you will decide to see people in how God sees them, and that's valuable and worthy. No one is asking you to agree with anyone's values or lifestyles. You are being asked to stop justifying putting yourself first because you think others around you are not equal to you.

How?
Take time to learn their story to understand who people are as individuals.
Ignore stereotypes or assumptions about people.
Listen to people, without judgment.
Give and do from a place of empathy and not sympathy.

You may learn you have a lot in common. You may also realize you may have what he/she need to change negative behaviors or that person may have what you need to achieve a goal or better your life. Just know people can glean from each other when they are not being belittled.

SELF CARE – Day 5 -7

Read over day 1 – 4 from this week and think about what you can do this weekend for yourself to help you celebrate strengthening your inner core. You did a lot of work this week to better yourself by completing KNOW YOUR VALUE days 1-4. Stay excited because you're ~~are~~ learning a lot! Take time to celebrate yourself. If you like, consider selecting an activity from the Self-Care Action Steps section on pages 27 -30 out of the book "How To Show Yourself Compassion - Get Rid Of Barriers To Self-Care." Please answer the questions below.

What did you decide to do? _____

Which day(s) are you going to do it? _____

How do you think taking care of yourself this way will benefit you in valuing yourself and valuing others?

_____
_____
_____
_____
_____
_____
_____
_____
_____

What do you believe about yourself on today (state a short affirmation)?

_____
_____
_____
_____
_____

Please repeat this affirmation all weekend and the following week to help you believe it from your heart and not just in your mind.

Remember to open this workbook on Monday to start the next lesson, enjoy your weekend!!

WORKBOOK for How To Show Yourself Compassion - Get Rid Of Barriers To Self-Care. (KNOW YOUR VALUE)

How to Value Self!

HOW TO VALUE SELF – Day 1

Please read the "How To Value Self" section from the book on page 15. Dr. Leath provided five steps to show you how to value yourself. Let's look at Step 1:

Accept who you are at this time, and accept the areas you can and cannot change

What areas about yourself do you wish you could change?

_____
_____
_____
_____
_____
_____

What will happen to you if those areas in your life never change?

_____
_____
_____
_____
_____
_____

What will happen to you if those areas in your life changed today or tomorrow?

_____
_____
_____
_____
_____
_____

Is there anything you can do to change it and not cause you or anyone harm?

_____
_____
_____
_____
_____
_____

Would people who love you agree with changing your life and be willing to help you? If your answer is yes, ask for their help and take steps to make those changes. If no, please go to the next question.

_____

_____

_____

You don't have the means to change what you don't like about your life and people in your life cannot help you with the process, what will it take for you to accept this part of your life?

_____

_____

_____

_____

_____

_____

Please understand everyone in the world has something in their life that they don't have the power to change. The only way to move forward, thrive, and not become stuck on that lack of control is to accept that you are powerless. Instead of denying your feelings about not being able to change things in your life you allow yourself to feel the sadness or anger. Only you can decide when you are ready to stop feeling sad or angry about who you are or your situation. The moment you decide enough is enough, you will reach out to people who can help you with acceptance. You will build relationships with people to help you understand in how to live in a way you can show yourself self-care and thrive as an individual. You will seek to see the good in who you are and your situation. You will be able to talk about how your perception has changed, which allowed you to move forward as you take one moment at a time.

There are also matters people can change about their lives, but don't believe it's possible. The moment the person thinks they cannot change or accept a situation, it's very difficult for a person to honestly change. They won't take steps, even with help, relapse and go back to their old habits, sabotage themselves to make sure they are right back where they started. Or they will talk about wishing they could do something and even have jealousy towards others who are accomplishing the thing in which they cannot do for whatever reasons. If this is you, all you would need to do is change your belief system about yourself. Start by being around people who you will like to become. Take time to learn from them, even if you have to pay for it. Always maintain respect for this person even after seeing their weaknesses. Research states that you become who you spend most of your time with and whom you admire. If you applaud the actions of a thief and spend a lot of time around thieves, most likely you will become a thief. So choose your crowd wisely.

Read aloud

"Today I, _____ will change the things I can change and accept the things I cannot. I will accept myself for who I am today and what I want for my future or my past failures. I am valuable because God created me and he gave me value. Nothing I do or say can remove that value. I'm thankful that I'm here and today I will care for myself and show myself compassion."

Step 2: *"Live authentically by knowing your deal breakers in relationships, jobs, clothing, even the quality of food you will eat."* What are your deal breakers for

Relationships?

_____
_____
_____
_____

Jobs?

_____
_____
_____
_____

Clothing?

_____
_____
_____
_____

Food?

_____
_____
_____

When do you override your deal breakers?

_____
_____
_____
_____

It is very important to have boundaries and know what you like and dislike. Then this way others won't be able to control you. Take time to get to know yourself unapologetically. Talk about what you want in a partner, what food you want to stay away from, or how you like to dress. If your reasons for your why are not healthy, be open to change, but still take time to know what you like and why then accept yourself for it.

HOW TO VALUE SELF – Day 3

Step 3: *"Forgive yourself for past mistakes, for how you have viewed yourself, and forgive others who caused you to feel unworthy"*

You already completed this step in the past two chapters so we are going to review the next step from the book.

Step 4: "Celebrate your peculiarities, knowing that you are unique; one of a kind and no one can be you."

List the things that make you different than most people.

_____
_____
_____
_____
_____

What made you shamed about your peculiarities in the past or today?

_____
_____
_____
_____
_____

What are you willing to do to accept your differences?

_____
_____
_____
_____
_____

Write down below why you are thankful for being different.

_____
_____
_____
_____
_____

HOW TO VALUE SELF – Day 4

Step 4: "Tell yourself who you are with positive affirmations daily."

Right now, you should have created two affirmations for yourself and was encouraged to say them daily. Today, please write your bio and discuss how wonderful you are to yourself and the people in your life. What will God say about you if you were allowed to see a video of your life today? What are your motives for helping and giving to others? Please be very honest with yourself. If you don't like your why for who you are, the great thing is you still have time to change your motives, but never stop doing good.

_____
_____
_____
_____
_____
_____
_____
_____
_____
_____
_____
_____
_____
_____
_____
_____
_____
_____
_____
_____
_____
_____
_____
_____
_____
_____
_____
_____
_____

HOW TO VALUE SELF – Day 5 -7

Read over day 1 – 4 from this week and think about what you can do this weekend for yourself to help you celebrate strengthening your inner core. You did a lot of work this week to better yourself by completing the HOW TO VALUE SELF days 1-4. Stay excited because you are learning a lot! Take time to celebrate yourself. If you like, consider selecting an activity from the Self-Care Action Steps section on pages 27 -30 out of the book "How To Show Yourself Compassion - Get Rid Of Barriers To Self-Care." Please answer the questions below.

What did you decide to do? _____

Which day(s) are you going to do it? _____

How do you think taking care of yourself this way will benefit you?

_____
_____
_____
_____
_____
_____
_____
_____
_____

What do you believe about yourself on today (state a short affirmation)?

_____
_____
_____
_____
_____

Please repeat this affirmation all weekend and the following week to help you believe it from your heart and not just in your mind.

Remember to open this workbook on Monday to start the next lesson, enjoy your weekend!!

GUILT

GUILT – Day 1

What can you do for yourself to get rid of your guilt for anything in your life, including showing self-care:

Spiritually?

_____
_____
_____
_____
_____
_____

Mentally?

_____
_____
_____
_____
_____
_____

Physically?

_____
_____
_____
_____
_____
_____

Emotionally?

_____
_____
_____
_____
_____
_____

Why is it important for you to get rid of your guilt?

_____
_____

GUILT – Day 2

Take time to identify people who cause you to feel guilty for showing yourself self-care and why (You will need to read the section in book about Guilt to understand this question).

Person 1

_____
_____
_____
_____

Person 2

_____
_____
_____
_____

Person 3

_____
_____
_____
_____

Person 4

_____
_____
_____
_____

Person 5

_____
_____
_____
_____

Person 6

_____
_____
_____
_____

GUILT – Day 3

Get rid of any forms of guilt today for showing yourself self-care.

Today I_____ let go of guilt of _____

_____
_____
_____
_____
_____
_____
_____
_____
_____

Why is it important to understand and believe that self-care is not a privilege for you?

_____
_____
_____
_____
_____
_____
_____

Why is it healthy to take care of yourself and put your physical, social and emotional needs first moreover? What must you do to make you provide yourself with self-care?

_____
_____
_____
_____
_____
_____
_____

GUILT – Day 4

Let someone know your needs – share your needs with your children, spouse, friend, or colleague. Inform them that you are feeling overwhelmed and you need time for yourself. Let them know what you are willing to do to make sure you maintain your responsibilities or give them time to prepare while you regroup. List the people below of who you need to inform and put a check by their names after you tell them you need to show yourself self-care.

_____

_____

_____

_____

_____

_____

Now that you have identified people and informed them of your needs, how did you feel afterwards?

_____

_____

_____

_____

_____

How would their response stop you or motivate you to give yourself self-care?

_____

_____

_____

_____

Write yourself a letter of why it is important to show yourself self-care even with the feelings of guilt.

Dear _____

_____

_____

_____

_____

_____

_____
_____
_____
_____

I love Me!

GUILT – Day 5 -7

Read over day 1 – 4 from this week and think about what you can do this weekend for yourself to help you celebrate strengthening your inner core. You did a lot of work this week to better yourself by completing GUILT days 1-4. Don't forget to take the time to celebrate yourself. If you like, consider selecting an activity from the Self-Care Action Steps section on pages 27 -30 out of the book "How To Show Yourself Compassion - Get Rid Of Barriers To Self-Care." Please answer the questions below.

What did you decide to do? _____

Which day(s) are you going to do it? _____

How do you think taking care of yourself this way will benefit you?

_____
_____
_____
_____
_____
_____
_____
_____
_____
_____

What do you believe about yourself on today (state a short affirmation)?

_____
_____
_____
_____
_____

Please repeat this affirmation all weekend and the following week to help you believe it from your heart and not just in your mind.

Remember to open this workbook on Monday to start the next lesson, enjoy your weekend!!

SELF-CARE IS

>NEEDED<

YOU CAN'T MAKE

SOMEONE

Care

. . . .

YOU CAN'T MAKE SOMEONE CARE – Day 1

Many people feel unappreciated by their spouses, children, or anyone they provide a service and don't get paid. Sometimes "Thank you" is not enough, or friends/family members may expect favors from you and not ask you your cost. Then you have people in your life who desire a big break or deal, even when they can afford to pay you for your services. You realize people you love may not care about you having the best experiences in life, but use you to thrive. This doesn't always feel good, especially when these same people become frustrated when you tell them no or need to take a break to give yourself self-care. How do you handle these types of people in your life?

_____
_____
_____
_____
_____
_____

Have you ever tried to make someone care about your wellbeing? If yes, how did that turn out?

_____
_____
_____
_____
_____
_____

Why should you not expect people to understand what you need?

_____
_____
_____
_____
_____
_____

When is it ok for another person in your life not to care about your wellbeing?

_____
_____
_____
_____
_____
_____

Why is it your responsibilities to make sure you care for self, even others don't see the need?

_____
_____

WORKBOOK for How To Show Yourself Compassion - Get Rid Of Barriers To Self-Care.(YOU CAN'T MAKE SOMEONE CARE)

YOU CAN'T MAKE SOMEONE CARE – Day 2

Take time to identify people you need to forgive you don't feel appreciation from, expect deals/favors from you, or don't take time to say Thank you. State their names, why you decided to forgive them on today, and what you are going to do next (accept it from them or let them how you feel in order to stop the behaviors).

Person 1

_____
_____
_____
_____

Person 2

_____
_____
_____
_____

Person 3

_____
_____
_____
_____

Person 4

_____
_____
_____
_____

Person 5

_____
_____
_____
_____

Person 6

_____
_____
_____
_____

YOU CAN'T MAKE SOMEONE CARE – Day 3

There are times in our lives; we feel like the victim without realizing we can also be who we judge or dislike about others. Identify people in your life who care about you by their actions and what do you do to show your appreciation. Also, state if you feel like you are doing enough or need to do more.

Person 1

_____
_____
_____
_____

Person 2

_____
_____
_____
_____

Person 3

_____
_____
_____
_____

Person 4

_____
_____
_____
_____

Person 5

_____
_____
_____
_____

Person 6

_____
_____
_____
_____

YOU CAN'T MAKE SOMEONE CARE – Day 4

People in your life want to care, but sometimes you may give mix messages. If they offer to help, you may say "I got it" or "I'm ok!" Even though you may not need their help or you can do it if a person is asking to help you, let them. Many people don't offer to help or don't say thank you over a period because they were trained not to by that person. Think about the times you said, "that's ok, you didn't have to say or do__" you are telling that person they do not have to appreciate you or offer to help you, so over time, they will stop. Why is it important for you to say "Thank you, yes please help me, I will appreciate that?"

_____
_____
_____
_____

What cause you or others to reject compliments or help?

_____
_____
_____
_____

Let's Practice!

Hello, you look nice today! (State how you will accept the compliment)

_____
_____
_____
_____
_____

Thank you so much for helping me with that project, I don't know what I would do without you! (State how you will respond)

_____
_____
_____
_____

Let me get that door for you or help you carry those items, you have a lot of things in your hands! (You know and trust this person – they are not trying to steal from you)

_____
_____
_____
_____

WORKBOOK for How To Show Yourself Compassion - Get Rid Of Barriers To Self-Care.(YOU CAN'T MAKE SOMEONE CARE)

YOU CAN'T MAKE SOMEONE CARE – Day 5 -7

Read over day 1 – 4 from this week and think about what you can do this weekend for yourself to help you celebrate strengthening your inner core. You did a lot of work this week to better yourself by completing YOU CAN'T MAKE SOMEONE CARE days 1-4. Don't forget to take time to celebrate yourself, because you are doing well. If you like, consider selecting an activity from the Self-Care Action Steps section on pages 27 -30 out of the book "How To Show Yourself Compassion - Get Rid Of Barriers To Self-Care." Please answer the questions below.

What did you decide to do? _____

Which day(s) are you going to do it? _____

How do you think taking care of yourself this way will benefit you?

_____
_____
_____
_____
_____
_____
_____
_____
_____
_____

What do you believe about yourself on today (state a short affirmation)?

_____
_____
_____
_____
_____

Please repeat this affirmation all weekend and the following week to help you believe it from your heart and not just in your mind.

Remember to open this workbook on Monday to start the next lesson, enjoy your weekend!!

WORKBOOK for How To Show Yourself Compassion - Get Rid Of Barriers To Self-Care.(YOU CAN'T MAKE SOMEONE CARE)

Figure Out Your Needs

FIGURE OUT YOUR NEEDS – DAY 1

It is very important to feel good about yourself when implementing self-care. When you do not feel good about yourself, it's easy to think that there's something fundamentally wrong with you. It feels deeply rooted and unchangeable, which is a false thought. In reality, you have not taken the time to clarify and pursue exactly what you need. Let's take time to examine what you need in all areas of your life. Take your time and don't rush this process. Write down what you need and what you are willing to do to make sure you gain it.

Spiritually?

_____
_____
_____
_____
_____
_____

Mentally?

_____
_____
_____
_____
_____
_____

Physically?

_____
_____
_____
_____
_____
_____

Emotionally?

_____
_____
_____
_____
_____
_____

FIGURE OUT YOUR NEEDS – Day 2

Let's get creative!
Below draw a picture of how you feel about yourself on today. Don't worry about how it looks, but do your best.

Draw a picture of how you will like to feel about yourself on today.

What do you need to do that is realistic to become how you want to feel or be?
_____
_____
_____
_____
_____
_____

WORKBOOK for How To Show Yourself Compassion - Get Rid Of Barriers To Self-Care. (FIGURE OUT YOUR NEEDS)

FIGURE OUT YOUR NEEDS – Day 3

What do you want to do with your life?

List the places you will like to travel.

_____
_____
_____
_____
_____
_____

List people you will like to meet.

_____
_____
_____
_____
_____
_____

What activities will you like to experience?

_____
_____
_____
_____
_____
_____

What Items will you like to have?

_____
_____
_____
_____
_____
_____

What are you willing to do to make these things happen in your life?

_____
_____
_____
_____
_____
_____

WORKBOOK for How To Show Yourself Compassion - Get Rid Of Barriers To Self-Care. (FIGURE OUT YOUR NEEDS)

WORKBOOK for How To Show Yourself Compassion - Get Rid Of Barriers To Self-Care. (FIGURE OUT YOUR NEEDS)

FIGURE OUT YOUR NEEDS – Day 4

You are responsible for your happiness and caring for yourself, why is that true?

_____
_____
_____
_____
_____
_____

Why do some people try to give others this power or expect others to make them happy?

_____
_____
_____
_____
_____
_____

When is the right time to include people in life to HELP with your happiness?

_____
_____
_____
_____
_____
_____

These questions are important because they help with maintaining balance concerning self-care. There are times you do need to include people when you are providing self-care, but you cannot depend on people to cause you to feel happiness during those times. You decide what makes you happy or unhappy. The more you learn what you dislike and like, you will be able to identify what you need.

FIGURE OUT YOUR NEEDS – Day 5-7

Read over day 1 – 4 from this week and think about what you can do this weekend for yourself to help you celebrate strengthening your inner core. You did a lot of work this week to better yourself by completing FIGURE OUT YOUR NEEDS days 1-4. Don't forget to take the time to celebrate yourself, because you are doing well. If you like, consider selecting activities from the Self-Care Action Steps section on pages 27 -30 out of the book "How To Show Yourself Compassion - Get Rid Of Barriers To Self-Care." Please answer the questions below.

What did you decide to do? _____

Which day(s) are you going to do it? _____

How do you think taking care of yourself this way will benefit you?
_____
_____
_____
_____
_____
_____
_____
_____
_____

What do you believe about yourself on today (state a short affirmation)?
_____
_____
_____
_____
_____

Please repeat this affirmation all weekend and the following week to help you believe it from your heart and not just in your mind.

Remember to open this workbook on Monday to start the next lesson, enjoy your weekend!!

WORKBOOK for How To Show Yourself Compassion - Get Rid Of Barriers To Self-Care. (FIGURE OUT YOUR NEEDS)

You shouldn't wait to be

valued you
should know you
are valuable

MAKE

TIME

MAKE TIME – Day 1

At the end of each session, you have been encouraged to implement self-care activities during your weekends, not knowing by completing these daily lessons in this workbook you have also been performing self-care according to our wonderful definition of self-care. This is awesome, but you are almost finished with this workbook so let's discuss how you can keep self-care happening in your life every day.

When do you have time alone during the day?

_____
_____
_____
_____
_____
_____

When are you open to spend time with others just to have fun?

_____
_____
_____
_____
_____
_____

From your answers, you can schedule when and the type of self-care activities you can implement in your life daily. The book suggested that you "Take time for yourself the second you wake up. Upon waking try: meditating, praying, reading, working out, or whatever you need to do to focus on providing yourself self-care spiritually, physically, emotionally, or mentally." (Leath, pg. 23) This is a great suggestion if you wake up on time or not late for work. You have to decide the best self-care activities that will fit your lifestyle. What are your suggestions?

_____
_____
_____
_____
_____
_____

MAKE TIME – Day 2

Create your schedule for self-care based off your responses on yesterday. What time and what will you do?

Monday

_____
_____
_____
_____

Tuesday

_____
_____
_____
_____

Wednesday

_____
_____
_____
_____

Thursday

_____
_____
_____
_____

Friday

_____
_____
_____
_____

Saturday

_____
_____
_____
_____

Sunday

_____
_____

WORKBOOK for How To Show Yourself Compassion - Get Rid Of Barriers To Self-Care. (MAKE TIME)

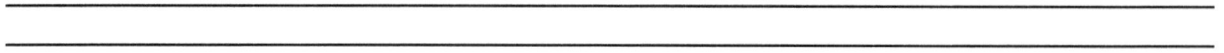

MAKE TIME – Day 3

The book suggest that you also provide self-care while on vacation. This is important to do, to make sure you return home refreshed and not needing another vacation. What can you do to make sure you provide self-care while on vacation?

_____
_____
_____
_____

How would the wrong people going with you on vacation prevent you from showing self-care?

_____
_____
_____
_____

What self-care activities can you do while on vacation?

_____
_____
_____
_____

Please make a sound decision today to never stop providing self-care even while on vacation. Why? Because to help and give of yourself to others, it is important that you are taking care of yourself in order to offer your best to others.

MAKE TIME – Day 4

"I don't have enough time, because....." This is the excuse we give ourselves when we don't want to make time. You do what you want to do and what you think is important. Today you need to know you are important and self-care is essential and non-negotiable. What are you willing to do to help yourself believe this about self-care?

_____

_____

_____

_____

There is a man name Jesus Christ in the Bible who prayed daily and even removed himself from people, food, and work to spend time with God, which is self-care. How do you think this impacted his life overall?

_____

_____

_____

_____

How do you think self-care will impact your life overall?

_____

_____

_____

_____

_____

MAKE TIME – Day 5 -7

Read over day 1 – 4 from this week and think about what you can do this weekend for yourself to help you celebrate strengthening your inner core. You did a lot of work this week to better yourself by completing MAKE TIME days 1-4. Don't forget to take time to celebrate yourself, because you are doing well. If you like, consider selecting an activity from the Self-Care Action Steps section on pages 27 -30 out of the book "How To Show Yourself Compassion - Get Rid Of Barriers To Self-Care." Please answer the questions below.

What did you decide to do? _____

Which day(s) are you going to do it? _____

How do you think taking care of yourself this way will benefit you?

_____
_____
_____
_____
_____
_____
_____
_____
_____
_____

What do you believe about yourself on today (state a short affirmation)?

_____
_____
_____
_____
_____

Please repeat this affirmation all weekend and the following week to help you believe it from your heart and not just in your mind.

Remember to open this workbook on Monday to start the next lesson, enjoy your weekend!!

It is imperative that you know your value and understand what it means to value yourself and others

CREATE YOUR *Affirmations*

1
Week 1
SELF-CARE

_____
_____
_____
_____

2
Week 2
KNOW YOUR VALUE

_____
_____
_____
_____

3
Week 3
HOW TO VALUE SELF

_____
_____
_____
_____

4
Week 4
GUILT

_____
_____
_____
_____

5
Week 5
YOU CAN'T MAKE SOMEONE CARE

_____
_____
_____
_____

6
Week 6
FIGURE OUT YOUR NEEDS

_____
_____
_____
_____

7
Week 7
MAKE TIME

_____
_____
_____
_____

8
Week 8
DO IT

_____
_____
_____
_____

ONCE YOU EMBRACE INVESTING IN YOURSELF AND BEGIN TO PRACTICE SELF-CARE, THE BENEFITS WILL QUICKLY BECOME APPARENT.

Commitment To Self-Care

I _____ make a commitment on _____ (date) to show myself self-care. I cannot expect others to care for me. I am responsible for caring for myself. I let go of all my excuses, guilt, or all reasons I use to not care for myself. I will do what's needed daily, because I matter and I am very valuable.

Print your name _____

Sign your name _____

LIVE

SELF-CARE

HELP

SELF-CARE

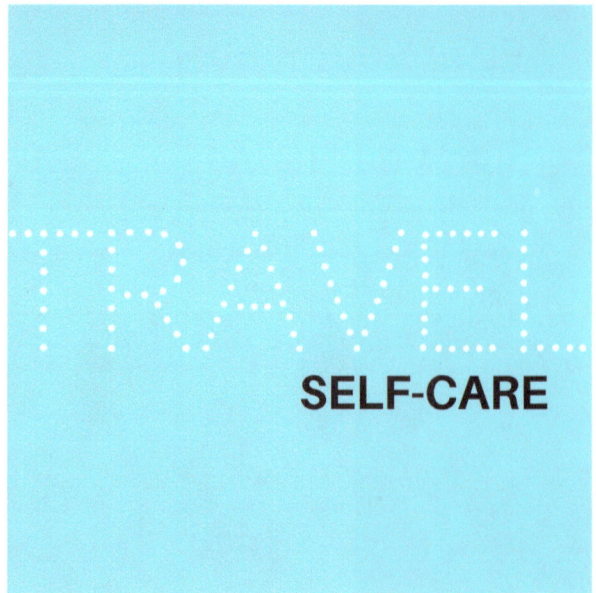

TRAVEL

SELF-CARE

www.ingramcontent.com/pod-product-compliance
Lightning Source LLC
Chambersburg PA
CBHW060828270326
41931CB00003B/104